Shekhinah

Phoenix Poets
A Series Edited by Robert von Hallberg

Shekhinah
Eleanor Wilner

The University of Chicago Press
Chicago and London

Eleanor Wilner is the author of *maya*, which received the 1979 Juniper Prize for poetry from the University of Massachusetts Press, and *Gathering the Winds*, a study of visionary imagination. She is a former editor of *The American Poetry Review* and a contributing editor for *Calyx*. Wilner's poems have appeared in numerous periodicals, including *Poetry*, *Ms.*, *The New Republic*, *Mother Jones*, *Epoch*, and *The Minnesota Review*, and in anthologies, most recently *Four Contemporary Poets*.

The University of Chicago Press, Chicago 60637
The University of Chicago Press, Ltd., London
© 1984 by The University of Chicago
All rights reserved. Published 1984
Printed in the United States of America

93 92 91 90 89 88 87 86 85 84   54321

Library of Congress Cataloging in Publication Data

Wilner, Eleanor.
  Shekhinah.

  (Phoenix poets)
  I. Title. II. Series.
PS3573.I45673S5 1984   811'.54   84-2511
ISBN 0-226-90025-8 (cloth)
      0-226-90026-6 (paper)

For my father
and in memory of my mother—
my luck in the beginning

Acknowledgments

"Emigration" first appeared in *MS.* (June, 1980); "The Refusal" (as "The White Imposture," earlier version) in *Calyx*, 3, no. 3 (February, 1979); "See-Saw" and "Caryatids" in *Calyx* 4, no. 1 (June, 1979); "The Uses of the Trellis" in *Calyx* 6, no. 1 (June, 1981); "My Mother's Portrait," in *The Goucher Quarterly*, 58, no. 1 (Fall, 1979); "Emily Brontë," "Without Regret," and "So Quietly the World" in *The Midwest Poetry Review* 1, no. 1 (Fall, 1980); "The English Department," "Cancelling the Space Program," "Reading *Frankenstein* at the Equator," and "Eris, the Goddess of Discord" in *The Midwest Poetry Review* 1, no. 2 (Summer, 1981); "Eleusis," "Candied," "Hunting Manual," and "Meditation on the Wēn-Fu" in *The American Poetry Review* 10, no. 6 (Nov./Dec., 1981); "Elegy for a Writer," *Cat's Eye* (Winter, 1981), reprinted in *Feminist Studies* 10, no. 1 (Spring, 1984); "How to Keep Teaching When You Can No Longer Define Romanticism," *Epoch*, 32, no. 1 (Fall, 1982); "Desertsong" (as "Womansong") in *The Painted Bride Quarterly*, no. 18 (Winter, 1983); "The End of the Line," "Recovery," and "The Continuous is Broken, and Resumes" in *The Third Wind* 1, no. 1 (Winter, 1983); "The Daughters of Midas," in *Chicago Review*, 34, no. 3 (Winter, 1984).

Thanks to Raphael Patai for "The Withdrawal of the Shekhinah from Her Home in the Temple," © 1967 by Rafael Patai. Reprinted from *The Hebrew Goddess* by Raphael Patai, by permission of KTAV Publishing House, Inc., New York, N.Y.

The Withdrawal of the Shekhinah from Her Home in the Temple

from the ark cover she moved onto the Cherub
from the Cherub onto the other Cherub
from the second Cherub onto the threshold of the Temple
from the threshold into the court of the Priests
from the court onto the altar in the court
from the altar onto the roof of the Temple
from the roof onto the wall
from the wall into the city of Jerusalem
from the city onto the Mount of Olives
from the Mount of Olives into the desert

Yehuda ben Idi (Hebrew, 3rd/4th century A.D.),
translated by Raphael Patai

My mother is dead . . . Icarus, Merope, Minos. My sister is a slave. My son will be an Attic killer. And our story, like all the others, is being told by liars. That is why I must write this for you. So that you will know what really happened. So that you will listen for Her voice.

June Rachuy Brindel, *Ariadne*

That glad, happy air, that winsome sky, did at last stroke and caress him; the stepmother world, so long cruel—forbidding—now threw affectionate arms round his stubborn neck, and did seem to joyously sob over him, as if over one, that however willful and erring, she could yet find it in her heart to save and to bless. From beneath his slouched hat Ahab dropped a tear into the sea; nor did all the Pacific contain such wealth as that one wee drop.

Starbuck saw the old man; saw him, how he heavily leaned over the side; and he seemed to hear in his own true heart the measureless sobbing that stole out of the centre of the serenity around.

Herman Melville, "The Symphony," *Moby Dick*

Silam or Silam inua, "the inhabitant or soul of the universe," is never seen; its voice alone is heard. "All we know is that it has a gentle voice like a woman, a voice 'so fine and gentle that even children cannot become afraid.' What it says is: *sila ersinarsinivdluge*, 'be not afraid of the universe.' "

The Eskimo shaman Najagneq, quoted by Joseph Campbell, *The Masks of God*

Contents

I. Revisions

Emigration

There are always, in each of us,
these two: the one who stays,
the one who goes away—
Charlotte, who stayed in the rectory
and helped her sisters die in England;
Mary Taylor who went off to Australia
and set up shop with a woman friend.
"Charlotte," Mary said to her, "you are all
like potatoes growing in the dark."
And Charlotte got a plaque in Westminster
Abbey; Mary we get a glimpse of
for a moment, waving her kerchief
on the packet boat, and disappearing.
No pseudonym for her, and nothing
left behind, no trace
but a wide wake closing.

Charlotte stayed, and paid and paid—
the little governess with the ungovernable
heart, that she put on the altar.
She paid the long indemnity of all
who work for what will never wish them well,
who never set a limit to what's owed
and cannot risk foreclosure. So London
gave her fame, though it could never
sit comfortably with her at dinner—
how intensity palls when it is
plain and small and has no fortune.

When she died with her unborn child
the stars turned east
to shine in the gum trees of Australia,
watching over what has sidetracked evolution,
where Mary Taylor lived
to a great old age, Charlotte's letters in a box
beside her bed, to keep her anger hot.

God bless us everyone until we sicken,
until the soul is like a little child
stricken in its corner by the wall; so there is
one who always sits there under lamplight
writing, staying on, and one
who walks the strange hills of Australia,
far too defiant of convention for the novels
drawn daily from the pen's "if only"—
if only Emily had lived,
if only they'd had money, if only
there had been a man who'd loved them truly . . .
when all the time there had been
Mary Taylor, whom no one would remember
except she had a famous friend named Charlotte
with whom she was so loving-angry,
who up and left to be a woman
in that godforsaken outpost past
the reach of fantasy, or fiction.

Without Regret

At first, we let them in. The heaven words worked
down, down the mineshaft
to the inner ear, where they hung, earrings
hooked in the winding flesh, rubies
ringing in the deep caverns,
in the darkest heart of what we heard.
While the waves went on breaking
at the cave's door, murmuring, we were
heaped like glitter on Holdfast's hoard.
He took us as he took the men for war.

Nights, by the light of whatever would burn:
tallow, tinder and the silken rope
of wick that burns slow, slow
we wove the baskets from the long gold strands
of wheat that were another silk: worm soul
spun the one, yellow seed in the dark soil, the other.

The fields lay fallow, swollen with frost,
expectant winter. Mud clung to the edges
of our gowns; we had hung back like shadows
on the walls of trees and watched. In the little circles
that our tapers threw, murdered men rose red
in their clanging armor, muttered
words that bled through the bars
of iron masks: the lord
who sold us to the glory fields, lied.

Trumpets without tongues, we wove lilies
into the baskets. When they asked us
what we meant by these, we'd say "mary, mary"
and be still. We lined the baskets on the sill
in the barn, where it is always dusk
and the cows smell sweet. Now the snow

sifts through the trees, dismembered
lace, the white dust of angels, angels.
And the ringing of keys that hang
in bunches at our waists, and the sound of silk
whispering, whispering.
There is nothing in the high windows
but swirling snow,
the glittering milk of winter.
The halls grow chill. The candles flicker.
Let them wait who will and think what they want.
The lord has gone with the hunt, and the snow,
the snow grows thicker. Well he will keep
till spring thaw comes. Head, hand, and heart—
baskets of wicker, baskets of straw.

Eleusis

Facts: March 6. Marianne Bachmeier, a barmaid,
walked into a Lubeck courtroom, fired six shots
and killed Klaus Grabowski, 35, accused of
molesting and strangling her 7-year-old daughter.
Grabowski had a long criminal record, including
sex offenses against young girls. In 1973 he
received a year's probation after trying to strangle a
6-year-old girl. In 1975 a judge, after finding him
guilty of sexually molesting two 9-year-olds, sent
him to a psychiatric hospital for a year. Marianne
Bachmeier, daughter of a member of Hitler's
Waffen-SS, is waiting to be tried for murder. The
West German Sunday paper, *Bild am Sonntag*, called
her, in a headline, "Mother Marianne."

The Law. The majesty of Law. "We are only
following orders."

In the countryside, where the crops are not yet
seeded in the ground, the earth shudders—
it opens yet another time, yawns
in some rapt exhaustion, and once again, in a swirl
of gravel, the sound of hoofs on stone,
the ruler rides, brother to the high god, Dis—
claiming the first flowers of the earth
he has divided. The land groans, and the women
weep, as they have always wept, as
the Father consents, the judges agree, the psychiatrists
nod their heads wisely and note
in German phrases in their little spiral books:
"He could not help himself; he had, no doubt,
a bad mother, an unresolved Oedipal complex.
Commit him to our care, and we shall set him free."

Crushed flowers in the wheel-rut on the road.
The voice of Hera coming down the years:
"If I cannot prevail upon the high gods,
I will stir up Hell." The clouds close in,
the light is strange and violet, almost
a bruise; Demeter tears her dark veil, tears
her long corn-colored hair, and stirs
the blood of Marianne, bearer of the cup,
the tarnished chalice, mother, murderess.
In her dreams, her little girl cries out,
cries out . . . the cry is endless as
the wars the Law allows: the vineyards
forever trampled under boots, the rumble
of the tanks replacing plows, the roar
of the chariot of Dis. He has split
the earth, the atom, the heart
of the world cracks—
and the petals look like scraps of silk
scattered in the dust. *Rape:* Old French
for the split skins and the stalks of grapes
after the wine has been pressed out.

And we were taught in school
how Roman law (and legions) brought
the world under a single rule; how
Greek men brought us closer to the sun,
the rule of light, annulling
the rule of blood for the pure, uneasy balance
of the Law. They blinded her—old Justice
with her bandaged eyes; set her, impartial, into stone
before the doors of courts, and sent

the Furies back, back into their caves
into the blood-red recess of the heart,
where they could only howl and tear
at their own flesh—no more to steal
the sleep of men or hound the killers
of their own kin and kind
until they fell upon the altars, spilled
like so much wine. So Death rode with the Law,
conscription took the young, and Justice,
in her marble robes, muttered *Pace, Pace,*
under her breath, and war led on to more,
death wholesale and life cheap; the buzzards
grew fat, more certain of their meat. Only
their necks, loose folds of hanging flesh, betrayed
them. The land put off the wearing of the green.

With a tearing sound, so like the tearing
of a young girl's flesh, Justice tears off her blindfold,
steps down from her perch of stone, her limbs
grow warm again, the live blood pulsing
through the marble veins . . . and Mother
Marianne loads her gun: six bullets, one
for each of the pomegranate seeds
that stained her daughter's mouth
with red. She throws her weight against
the courtroom doors, bursts in—burning
like a torch, a brand in the hand of Demeter—
and fires six shots at Klaus before the eyes
of a stunned court, and the children there
on an outing for their civics class.

"I sing of Demeter, the lovely haired, and of
her daughter, Kore, slender ankled, picking flowers
by the lake, and singing . . ."

Zeus gave her to his brother for his sport.
The time grows short; the wounds of earth are
gaping. Sisters, brothers, light
your torches and restore
the mysteries. The wheat is all the gold
we'll ever know, the earth our own, and only
sphere. A deeper law moves scarlet in its veins.
We are but nature given eyes, and by a twist
of DNA, earth given to our care.
As old men rage in all our capitals,
as the missiles shuttle on their tracks,
earth shudders and Persephone
is rising in the fields, and all the flowers—
as if the dumb, dishonored earth were given tongues—
cry out, cry out, cry out.

Eris, the Goddess of Discord

Too much Concord, not enough Discord.
    Margaret Fuller to her Transcendentalist friends
    Emerson, Thoreau, & co., of Concord, Massachusetts

Old, hackneyed as I am, I still remember when I was not
invited to the wedding—crossed desires—
a god's love denied a god and given to a man.
His warlike son swam restless in his loins,
her half of him still undisturbed, hidden
within the crimson folds of women's
garments, the first of many shields she would
provide him. Foolish woman, the ocean
was her home; she should have known.
She was part of the plot against me.
She should have heard my cackle
shake the pillared hall outside the bridal chamber,
Troy's fire crackling through the years,
the static behind the chamber music,
the string quartets of Bluebeard's castle,
a metaphysic playing over
the groans from the locked attic.
The curtain slightly lifted, their hackles rose
at me—the crack in the rose window, the wind
they shut their doors against.

They banned me from the schools as if no
chaos lurked under the black robes of dons,
but I swirled up in all the margins where
the scholars squabbled, tore
each other's careful arguments to bits.
Each time I throw my golden apple in,
they bicker on about beauty, the perfect argument
to bring those towers blazing to the ground,
charred swans and a ditch full of bleeding bronze.
The clouds brooding dark over the scene
like some Homeric eye. The dragging footsteps of the god
drag on. Sweet Vergil with his big black Latin tears
took pains to banish me, set me alight with Dido
on her pyre, and set the Roman phalanx like a wedge
into the world's heart. And the dark rain poured in
the oculus of the Pantheon, streaking the walls.
And when the spokes of that great Roman
wheel, on which so many lives were broken, broke—
Mary rode in from the provinces on an ass
and I was not invited to the christening.
The same mistake, the same witch burning at the stake.

Play the *Te Deum* again; behind it you will hear
the dice rattle, the din of tambourines
the gap-toothed gypsy dancing
in her rags, the bag ladies
with their quacking tongues
the bullets' hail on tin
the tin tin tin tinin tin tin
the hunchback drumming as the moon goes down.

          *   *   *

But oh, the baying of the hounds is music
to me; they bay for what their dog-souls love—
the heavy scent, the hills, to run
and make the air the vibrant echo of their tongues.
"I never heard so musical a discord, such sweet thunder."
The chase is long, the fox grows wiser with delay.
No rancor here, no one to give the bride away.

Candied

In Eden it was never winter, the ground
stayed wet and spongy, the sun as yellow
and as overripe as Persian melon, the streams
gummed up with honey, and the apples mushy:
how things had got so soft is hard to say.
Maybe just being naked in the woods
with chigger bites around your ankles
and stinging flies and deep infections
breathed in every cut by rotting matter,
and, staring from the bushes, boars,
stiff-bristled, with tusks that tear
through skin and gristle—this kind of thing
would scarcely do for starters.

No, it had to be sweet
as grass, the kind of stuff that's habit-
forming, like all things half-conceived:
for instance, Adam
anesthetized, and God, part surgeon, part
cosmic dating service,
taking her out for the first time
to see how it would go (the Bible
leaves this part out,
although the Greeks, not believing
in premature withdrawal, left it in.)

So I guess the way it ended was
that Eve got up, walked out
on Adam, their tacky Eden—sick
of honeysuckle, of trees stuck up
with signs to state their meaning,
and nothing to stick to your ribs
but apples—she'd had a bellyful
of those, an earful
of the chirping choir in the hedges, and
everything so blessed cheerful—
so she pushed past the flaming doorman,
headed out the road that unwound
like the wrappings of a mummy—that Eden
with its little sickly nightingales
the color of rancid butter, its flowers nodding
in continual agreement, its crickets and
its sticky, sticky rivers.

Emily Brontë

Cold in the earth, and the deep snow piled above thee!

Constant as the wind that lifts
sheer curtains from the sill, and fills
the room, and even the flame
of the well-trimmed lamp will flutter,
the dust will dance
before it settles, the dark outside
will utter its own cries—
a sighing of the oak's great branches rubbing sky
and a sound so hushed
it might be gray moss growing, inching slowly
over the churchyard stones, that paving
over hell—some carved with dates that say
short life, short life, while others
measure lives fourscore or more—
as if the lungs were made to breathe
the moors, the rain-drenched air, and quickly
sicken, fill and die; or else, outliving
all, to watch the others die.

When we climbed the winding hill
up through the village to the unprotected
crest where the wind is sovereign, unrelenting—
we came to the parsonage of stone
next to the graveyard, and the church
too small and gray to be called
charming. The huge trees towering over
headstones, drip with a damp
that works its way inside, past warming,
we follow the wind to the edge
of house and churchyard where it pours
desolate across the moors, wave on wave of monotone,
as bellows fill the organ and a solitary note swells out

and fades, swells out, forever. All gray—
the moors, the sky and fieldstones, the winter
sheep in cloudy wool, the gray stuff
that our lungs become, and that unearthly
pearl—the color of the brain, and homespun stuff
the sisters dressed in, for warmth and to discourage
questions. I see them making plans and whispering
in the night around the fire, their faces flushed
a strange, unwholesome red. Though Emily
I cannot see—she, like a passage left in Greek
on a page of English, speaking shadows
on a lamplit wall, the branches swaying
till the paper comes alive, the stones
open to a slash of sky
in which two stars are shining: twin soul
with a single pair of eyes.

A glimpse is all—then something dives
into the ink of nighttime waters, as she
moved hidden in their midst, invisible
as wind across a landscape made of rocks.
Nor did she seem to be there now
in Haworth, among those stones, unless
in silhouette against the gale,
her hair blown back as if
she would be wind and grass, the master
of herself, so she remains
a breathing there between the lines
of graves, a breathing
like a wolf-gray wind that howls
through all the passages left open in the stone.

The Refusal

Listen: the sound
of a gate creaking—it is Emily, trying to leave
her father's house. It is night in New England,
Amherst, where the air is purple with midnight,
bewitching, a plum the heart promised, rich
with juice and fit to burst—but
her hand falters on the gate, her breath catches
in her throat like a burr inhaled, a stuck
spur of sharp steel—and the sky
went hard as amethyst, and like a jewel
it shone—god, it shone so bright,
and she turned back, and shut the gate
so quietly that no one—unless it was her—
heard it click.   And maybe, climbing back
up those stairs again, to that room
that was waiting
like the rest of her life, it was like
climbing the sheer face of a granite cliff,
so high and the night below so deep,
so immeasurably deep, that each step
was a victory, a triumph over the law
of gravity that was all the time calling
the way parched earth cries out to the rain—
come down, come down, come down.

But she did not. She went up, and shut
the door. She sat down and wrote
and the words fell from her pen
like amethysts, precious and glowing with
congealed night—you could almost hear their brittle
rattle as they rolled across the floor, against
the door—but she, she thought she heard
death knocking, and she would not
get up again, she would not
go down, she would never
answer the door.

Listen, you can barely hear us
coming down the years, the brown slow stairs
on which the grass is grown thick and blurs
our long departure into summer air;
there, by the well, we stop and fill
the urns with blue water, an offering to pour
onto that awful mound,
that silent, stoppered roof.
Some part of you that now
bursts into bloom for us
knew better than believe this porous
earth would ever hold you
as you held yourself
aloof.

The World Is Not a Meditation

Odysseus, Penelope
that aging wife with a fixed idea—Odysseus.
Strange pair to put against the blare of sirens
on the news, prime time wars that flicker
through the brain—still, through it all:
one man lashed to a mast, one woman
tied by her own hair to a loom.

She nods a little at her work, her hands
fall idle in her lap. By now, she isn't sure
what she is waiting for; her mind
wanders, she has stopped
trying to comb the knots from her hair
nights, when the candles sputter
like some bright notion she's about
to lose. His seed is scattered
in so many nymphs, it's no surprise
that half the babies born
on distant islands look like him,
though they think different thoughts and
cannot bear his name. The son he spawned
in legal loins is out for him, inheritor
of his mother's fond obsession. The others
turn away from him, without a blink
of recognition—black eyes, exactly
his, but blank as the ripe olives
pressed for oil, that endless flow
that keeps the great wheels wet
and turning, cutting grooves across the back
of earth; everywhere, the burning towns.

Odysseus has returned. And the men
who sailed with him? All lost
or drowned. He's stopped his ears
so he won't hear them calling, men
tossed into the waves like coins
to appease some hypothetical Poseidon.
Their sound keeps breaking
on the shore—the voices of the drowned,
the unrenowned, the living tide
incessant, whispering: anonymous,
anonymous, anonymous . . . the foam
left on the stones when the waves
withdraw—transparent roe, ghost spawn,
it glitters for a moment and is gone.

It is the morning after
Odysseus' return. The suitors lie in heaps
like so much garbage, the flies
already thick. Outside the great gate
of his house on Ithaca, a wailing
like a siren call—the women
with their urns, empty, asking
for the ashes of their sons, their lovers,
something—even a word.
But the shutters of the great house stay closed
against the hot Greek sun. The women
turn at last and go, to glean
the fields, to make strange beds, whatever
kind of home they can invent.
Only Penelope holds her own man
in her arms, the man who left her
to her own thoughts all those years.
What she thinks now
is hers alone, Odysseus the intruder.

　　　　　*　　　　　*　　　　　*

For those who don't like endings, let the story lift
like ruffled feathers in the wind,
refuse to settle. And let
the not-quite fiction of Penelope
pick up another thread from deep inside her
where the nerves are taut along the bone,
her body like the lute when it is strummed,
from a house that's full
of signals: the slow foot of the cat
upon the stair, the roaches drinking
in the pipes, the hairs that seem to swim
in the washing water, the lizards
rustling in the leaves, the way
that even silence is alive
with premonitions.

Listen. The sound of scissors clicking.
One by one, she cuts the threads
that strung the loom. The shroud
that she'd been weaving
becomes a cloud of falling
shreds, till the room is littered
with useless threads, like sentences
from which the sense has fled.
She shakes her head as if to free it
from the name that she'd repeated
all those years, a litany
for the dead, or an aimless mantra
meant to cover dread—
that frame a gallows
where she had hung, a spider
strangling in its web.

The catch had rusted on the shutters
from disuse. She had to force it.
When she threw the shutters open
it was summer and the sun was high.
As her eyes adjusted to the brilliance
she saw the shape of things outside: a frieze
the wind set into motion, the fields
pouring like an ocean into distance,
the wind-stirred trees, the gate
like someone waiting, the winding road . . .

A knock came at the door and then repeated.
She threw the bolt to buy herself
the time she needed. When he had forced
the door, the room was empty and the loom
stood vacant by the open window.
The sun was blinding: the frame held
only light without an image.

It is not the business of another
to imagine any further. Once she has cut
the long threads of the story, its convenience—
she is free. Abuse *that* word at your peril,
it will return to mock you, like the nameless
who leave their names behind them—
the signatures that spell rebellion,
a freehand scrawl of bright graffiti
on the white, expensive wall.

The Uses of the Trellis
for Olga Broumas

Olga, reading you today, the first of February,
your Oregon landscape full
of its lost lover: all at once I mourned
the disappearance of the leaves.
Though yesterday, the same as you, I found their absence
welcome, wished them always gone
as if I were October and my breathing
might cool the land and strip
the trellis and the trees
down to their perfect architecture.

But our meanings like the shimmer
of reflected light on water, shift
and shift by nature, or from wind.
Then, too, the body
is so cryptic when it speaks
we follow it as dolphins playing
in the bow wake of a passing ship
until it strikes a hidden reef—
and words fall through the mind
as wrecks through the darkening water, aimless
as they tumble in slow motion, turning
till they jar against the soft mud
at the bottom, shudder and are still.
And though the cargo
borne down with them
is all lost, it isn't long
before the broken portholes
open into portals for the fish.

Today, I find myself reverting, perhaps
to type, and I regret the leaves
I tried to shed like Demeter in autumn
inconsolable and lonely for
her daughter, and taking it all out
on the good earth, stripping the trees as if
to bare the soul, as if the soul
were merely trellis
and the trees were only
scaffolds built to hang
the flesh, that flower in its velvet,
velvet leaves.

Concerto

I think of an early Christian
kicking off sandals and scratching, barefoot,
the shape of a fish in the sand.
And I think of the centuries passing, a long
torchlit procession down a corridor
of stone, lugging their armored dead, heavy
as the memory of Anchises on their backs.
And the outline of the fish effaced
by a passing wind, the earth bare dust
without an image, till at sea, miles out
from the jagged shadows
cast by the great cathedrals—
something leaps and makes a silver
bell sound in the sun . . .

this time, the little mermaid
waking from a fable with a start
has no desire for legs
to crawl up on the beach, to painfully
stand and walk the rough stones
to the castle, casting behind her
the wavering shadow of a fish.
This time she won't be standing
at the circle's edge to watch
the dancing figures: slim men in skintight
velvet, the women with their blossom
skirts that open as they turn;
out of her element, her new feet
raw, moving in her stockings
like live fish trapped in mesh.

Mayerling, Mayerling, the dancers turn
like figures on a German music box—a cunning
kind of verisimilitude, but wooden,
wooden: the music tinkling
like a shower of crystal in a hall of glass.
A picture in a fraying child's book,
its frame an etched black line, its caption:
"In the moonlit ballroom, how they danced."

Far down the beach, the fishermen
cast their nets; the sea pours through them.
She leaves her rock, the sun
behind her, dives back into her shadow
and as she parts the water, the long scar
of her leaving is healed in an instant.
At first, the gliding shapes are silent.
Though soon, as the legs
that she once longed for, grow
accustomed to their fusion,
as the shadowed lines along her ribs
begin to open like the slats
of a venetian blind to let in water,
the silver scales descending with her,
she will begin to hear
the pizzicato of her sonar striking
minnows, the long strings of the bow waves
drawn across the bridges till they hum,
the wild choirs of whales singing,
the deep ground bass of ocean moving,
her own small waving tail the obbligato.

So Quietly the World

I'm Nobody, Who are you?

Let them who love their names
in light, remember—
the journey into hell, the meeting
with the faceless, bandaged women
in the infirmary on the outskirts
of Saigon, Hiroshima: hands
reaching out to catch your skirt, then
through those flame-lit corridors
that turn and narrow, you
burn, the torch in the dream to light
your way back to the living . . .

sit down
the way the British Navy captain did, on the edge
of his bed in Bedlam, recovering
from psychosis, saying
his own name over and over
to end the nightmare
of the battle flares, too much
illumination—

as you say yours: anonymous.
not made to be the enemy of man,
not made to take
his name, but being one
who sheds
his fame, his self-important
naming, to state your own
unfinished, small, specific
business, so quietly the world
can still be heard
saying itself forever
over, like a prayer
the wind says as it turns
the birch leaves over, silver
or the light stir
of the dust
that goes on dancing
long after the feet that raised it
have gone by.

II. Retrospectives

The English Department

Here on England's further shore,
one of the oddities of evolution, the ovaries
of Darwin, holding the helical hopes
in pure solution: tomorrow, tomorrow and
tomorrow—suddenly yesterday. Phaëton come down
to take the waters, pallid cures
for what was coming after, an empire
taken with a gin
and tonic, Cordelia dead, too light
in the arms of Lear to be a body,
Ophelia forever floating
on the pond. Above, the emerald banks
where Shakespeare grazed, his huge eyes
gentle as a heifer's, his belly full of green,
a second stomach for another, greener
world: the one distills and feeds
the other. Now the green moss grows
on the sunless side of every cemetery marker.

In the parks the silent children play
like little men and women, their minds
lit up inside like William Morris windows,
the lurid glow of burning castles, a red-dressed
woman laughing on the rafters like a crow,
the great lord blind and poking in the ashes.
They live below in the lodge now, stained air
not quite salubrious, the garden gone to gravel.

You take your language where you get it,
sift it through the mind, the centuries,
like soil through a sieve, gathering the stones
in the silver meshes, letting the earth
go back to earth. Sweet gods, then let them
keep the stones and throw
the good rich dirt away, we'll back
to the ground again, before the first lance
split the air, tear out the Latin roots and paint
our bodies blue again to frighten the invaders—
unwrite the words and pour them
loud, the color of earth, on air
and in the ear for their deep sounding,
untranslatable as howls, moving as water,
round and momentary as the flowers, stars
to spur the pounding feet, the blackest sight,
darkness returning with the speed of light.

Hunting Manual

The unicorn is an easy prey: its horn
in the maiden's lap is an obvious
twist, a tamed figure—like the hawk
that once roamed free, but sits now, fat and
hooded, squawking on the hunter's wrist. It's easy
to catch what no longer captures
the mind, long since woven in,
a faded tapestry on a crumbling wall
made by the women who wore keys
at their waists and in their sleep came
hot dreams of wounded knights left bleeding
in their care, who would wake the next morning
groaning from the leftover lance in the groin,
look up into the round blonde face beaming down
at them thinking "mine," and say: "angel."
Such beasts are easy to catch; their dreams
betray them. But the hard prey is the one
that won't come bidden.

By these signs you will know it:
when you lift your lure
out of the water, the long plastic line
will be missing its end: the lure and the hook
will be gone, and the line will swing free
in the air, so light it will be without
bait or its cunning
sharp curl of silver. Or when you pull
your net from the stream, it will be eaten
as if by acid, its fine mesh sodden shreds.

Or when you go at dawn to check your traps,
their great metal jaws will be wrenched
open, the teeth blunt with rust
as if they had lain for years in the rain.
Or when the thunderstorm suddenly breaks
in the summer, next morning
the computer's memory will be blank.

Look then for the blank card, the sprung trap,
the net's dissolve, the unburdened
line that swings free in the air.
There. By day, go empty-handed to the hunt
and come home the same way
in the dark.

Cancelling the Space Program

What if the world were real?
And Sartre's nausea nothing
but the queasy stomach of the morning after
the long intoxication
of the mind, bent like a bow to send the spirit
into the gauzy reaches
of the clouds beyond the madhouse
on the slopes of Mt. Olympus. Till
like some laboratory in the sky
that tires of its orbit, it comes down
to find itself in ruins—
down under, in the outback of Australia
among strange animals who bear their young
too soon: raw, half-made things that
have to crawl to find a haven
high above them, in the pouch,
while they are blind. Transcendence.
That was the word, and how the heart
lifted, till it soared
up through the ceiling and, shattering
the skylight, headed for the stars.
And the poor soul, with broom in hand,
was left behind to sweep the splinters.
All winter, how the snow
sifted in through the broken skylight,
piling up like cast-off drafts
of poems, while through the ragged opening—
the changing sky: it taught us gravity,
how things come down, as objects fall
through water, as Arthur's sword
is always sinking
toward the bottom, toward the mud

where life is thickest and the fish
are feeding. That's why
we fish with sinkers on our lines,
the necessary weight that feels for
the telling thud that is the bottom.
While Henry David, all by himself
by Walden Pond, though half a mile
from his mother, could sit all day and gaze
at the reflection of the sky
and dream a pond without a bottom,
his mind high on the waters
of the Ganges where the Hindus
launch their countless dead, who float off—
lilies on their pads—till the water
has its way and drags them under.
Though later they will rise again
as a drowned man on the third day rises
to the surface, violates its calm—
a mirror, disturbed, that bulges
till it bursts, and damp distended forms
emerge, dragging weeds like chains
except that they are green and silent,
the human shape defying
recognition, blown out of all proportion,
the monstrous avatar
of Proteus, so slippery
that the hero's hand had lost its grip,
his chance to steady
the shape-changer
till he will come around again to being
human, the water playing mirror again,
intact, serene, reflective: our selves

worn lightly on the deep's own skin,
floating easy as a tired swimmer
lies back to feel the waves curl up beneath her,
steady, beating like a quiet heart,
and see above her—bending down
as if in greeting—
the sheltering arch of sky.

The Fourth David
for Bob who gave me the poem

I. Donatello 1430–32: 62¼"
He stands there sleek and calm
and dark in bronze, hardly more
than a boy, his stomach muscles
not yet hard. His poise is slightly
coy; he rests his left foot
on the fallen head as if
it were a hummock in the lawn, overgrown
with matted grass. Relaxed, withdrawn,
his flesh a speaking bronze, denies
base metal, says instead, but softly:
"please" and promises a pleasure
in its ease. His knees are slightly
bent, his hat is insolent, one soft
hand holds a stone as useless
as a flower; his sword might be
a Hermes wand, health to the unsuspecting.
Shape-changer, cool as the poplar's
shade at the cross-roads, he stands
above his shield as if he had no need
of it—nude, indolent as May
that ushers in a lassitude
the young have when they only dream
of fame. His name is David;
he wears it lightly as the air
wears dawn. His hair hangs loose,
as careless as men are before
they know how they arouse
the giant, out there,
drowsing naked in the sun.

II. Michelangelo 1501–4: 13' 5"
And now he feels the weight
of stone. His body, older, has grown
muscular and tense; he broods
the consequence of playing out
a part he never wanted, he who loves
the lyre and the lamb. He is enormous
in his sex, as if his power
were boulder-born, quarried by a hand
whose veins were throbbing with
a blood they barely could contain,
as if to act were risking floods
of red whose flow would make a river
meager. His pride demands
more than his heart can bear, Hamlet
standing in the hall by a tree stump
like an auger; doubt worms its way
across his brow and furrows it—
a freshly harrowed field
uncertain of its crop. He is a giant
who knows the power he holds in his hand
is only his until
he lets the stone go from the sling.

III. Bernini 1623: life-size
Stand back. The time is past
all hesitation. His eye is fixed: the enemy
is in its center—out there, in the space
he wants to enter; behind him you can hear
the awful anthems and the armies crowding out the light.
His face too set and sharp, too hard
to be a boy's; his sex is draped, his body
shaped now for a different use:
to loose the stone is all, his will
is stone, the figure poised to follow.
The sling is stretched, the rock
is in his hand, his body twisted with
the torsion of the throw.
All his force is focused on tomorrow's
crown; nothing will stop him now.
Intolerable to watch
the slow unfolding of the marble
arms and feel already in your bones
the body of the giant toppling
like a forest through the years
until it's sprawled out on a field
from which the shade's been hacked, the limbs
and trunk from which the leafy head
is missing—discarded weight
that once set matter into motion
and dreamed a ceiling with an infinite recession
of heavy angels toward a filmy light like God.

IV. Anonymous 1979
Bronze will not soon speak again
in such sweet tones, nor stone relent
before the sculptor's hand.
How long ago it seems, just past
the flood, the last surviving pair
obeyed the oracle of Themis and restored
the human form by throwing the bones
of earth, the stones, behind them
as they crossed the desolate and flood-torn
plain. And stone grew warm and turned
to flesh, its veins began to pulse
with life, and only something flinty
in the heart retained the memory
of stone, that David loosed—
dead aim, the king who set the stone
in history's sling, and time's
the long slow transit back to granite.

At the museum gate, mute pipes of iron
stand against the sky. Beside them,
on a shaft ten stories tall,
a mobile made of burnished steel
turns in the wind, and turns again
in the dark mirror of the museum wall.
A child, call him David,
plays nearby in the sand. He looks up once
at the towering iron art, these giants
of an alien design, and turns away
and takes his mother's hand
and says, in a voice too small for anyone
but her to understand, "now
can we go home?"

Metamorphoses at a College for Women
for Brooke Peirce

For years he had been staring at
a sea of girlish heads, bobbed hair
or page-boys sleek and turned under
as silk sheets on perfectly made
beds. They were, really, flawless
little Andromedas, chained to their
desks, taking notes and waiting
for a husband to come and rescue them.
Their smiles were melting, no stone
in their gaze. And the days passed
like the glazed landscapes on
a painted urn of porcelain, vaguely
Chinoise, a little out of any style.

He wasn't sure just when it was
he first saw it—perhaps
it was a tendril of hair
poking out of a smooth
wave, but suddenly it was
the way a wave curls just
before it breaks.
That's when he saw
the snakes he hadn't seen
before, twisting and
hissing at the fringes of his
vision—and he reached for his shield, and thought:
dear gods, not me.
There is more, after all,
than one kind of hero; there are those
who, after years of patiently looking,
when they suddenly see their luminous bronze
shield fill up with the face of
Medusa,
smile, put down the sword
and say: at last.

This time, when the dragon
slides out of the waves, belching
fire and girl-crazy as ever,
there'll be no one chained waiting
at the rock for his dinner, no one
with a double-edged sword to dismember
those gorgeous, glowing coils—
    only a bright sheen on the water
    a tumbled shore, and walking along it,
    an avid reader of Ovid with his book,
    and stretched out on her blanket in the sun
    a long-haired woman idly writing
    taking her dictation
    from the wind.

How to Keep Teaching When You Can No Longer Define Romanticism

Follow the dots. Those puzzle books
we had when we were children. Disappointing when
the picture was too easy to extract: you could see
what it would be before
you laid the pencil to the page. But, oh, the ones
that were a perfect mystery of dots, a clouds of gnats
that camouflaged a king, or anything
might suddenly emerge—a rabbit, or a demiurge—a certain
faith in what was hidden, designs assured us
by our pencils and the numbers: "the lineaments
of gratified desire," a silken luxury of sense.

That was, of course, before the points
were facts, stranded on a graph.
Before the first commercial interruption.
And I've forgot
the shape of constellations: the sky's
an anarchy of stars, as if some cosmic seamstress
spilled her sequins.

All those fox years gone to earth.
Each new career
a careful demolition of the last.
And never living long enough
in any house to see
the trees I planted grow to anything like shade.
I plant, now, annuals out of packets,
the scattered, separate seeds whose shape
depends no longer on relation: each one
with its own fond memories of marigold
locked in, each one a possible burst
of yellow. Each year I plant too late
for any hope of flower; each year
I'm still too soft
to do the thinning: who knows which one might
prove the stronger, and then the little ones
are so disarming. A gardener needs a mind
for larger figures. But never mind, I won't be home
with water when it's time
to see them through
the summer's heat, the storm of gnats, the long nights
when the thunder only threatens. And yet, there's that
relief when weeds take over, a random green
that cares as little for attrition as for care.
I could make a poetics of that, and some night
when I need to pull a rabbit out for class, I might.

A Short History of Philosophy

We're here because we're here because we're here
because . . .
Children's bus song, originally a WWI trench song

One day the elephant gets up and lumbers
to the pool, looks down, recoils—
what is this lumpish thing he sees, this vast
and gray assemblage of loose skin, the wrinkled
knees, the sad eyes sunk in flesh like dough,
enormous horny feet, the limp hose hanging
where his nose should be? And what
are those crescent moons of bone that rise
on both sides of his jaws? He trumpets once,
sits down, and mud spills out around him.

He'd seen this monstrous thing before—
his mate, the herd, the great
gray clowns he'd travelled with, but he
was not like them—for he moved easy through
the bush, could feel the earth shake under him—
such power, and how he loved
to take the water in and fire his silver geyser
at the sun. And he had been
a mountain crossed with wind, a landscape
set in motion by a wish, and from the deep
recesses of his brain, in drought,
he could summon up by memory alone
rain forests with their varnished leaves,
water falling through the dark and shining
green, the red hibiscus blooming with a splash
as if in answer to the brass
insistence of his booming Gabriel voice.

And, though slow to anger, once aroused
he could turn the other creatures like a tide
that ebbed away from his enraged approach.
He was the one who moved and, moving, made
the world around him run. And those he lived
among, though their ugly bodies made him sad, had
always seemed the price he paid for company,
the way the old gods sought the mortals out
for sport, then grieved for them who were
so clumsy, quarrelsome, and had to die.

Now, as he sat mourning by the pond, he knew
himself their kind, a huge and monstrous
clod of sodden mud. He cursed his great
remembering mind—a Plato by the waterhole,
descended from a great idea. And lost
in misery there, he hardly felt
the great net when it dropped, was
too absorbed to struggle when it caught
and he was hauled by derricks to the waiting
truck. And later he was taught to walk
by rote the little circus ring, to gather
all his weight upon a red upholstered stool
and turn while children laughed
and a lady in pink tights
made light of him by sitting in his trunk
as if it were a garden swing.

Sometimes late at night, he would look up
through the black slats of the boxcar
as it swayed and bounced along the tracks
and see the stars wink on and off, tilting
in the crazy sky that seemed so fugitive
as if, like him, it would fly towards a pond
in some lost forest in a greener world
and there, in silence, would look down
on a patch of stars at rest below, attended by
a swaying grace, gray matter, beautiful
as mind made flesh—at home
at last and looking up
from the quiet waters of the earth.

Backtracking

Some time at night when two trains pass—
it begins with a stir of air between the cars,
the faint whir of an alarm
just before it rings, then noise
like wings of steel brushing glass,
a pressure in the ears and down the spine, a blur
of lighted windows rushing past, a face
you recognize in an embrace—your own,
another's. Then it's past, someone
you lost and were, now ten years gone.
Stop it at your cost.

Here at the siding the two trains slow
and grind their brakes against complaining
wheels and halt. Alight
and pick your way across the tracks,
find the other car where it is parked,
the lighted window like a welcome in the dark.
This is what the memory-ravaged old
must see, the light they stop for, leaving
the stub with their destination stamped
in the little metal clamp above the seat,
to slip away unnoticed in the night
and board the train they used to ride,
lit when their own car's darkened for
the sleepers there inside.

I knock at the closed metal,
it slides back; I pause and hear
the racket of the insects by the tracks,
late summer voices magnified
as I climb inside—up the iron
stairs, into the vestibule, and push
the center square: the door
slips back into the wall—the lit car
waits before me.
The dread comes as it comes to those
who fear to view the corpse of one
who'd been their lion's share
of light. The choice
is this exactly: to tarnish silver
by exposing it to air, to bear
the superimposition of the lifeless thing
over the glowing life you'd shared, or
never to accede to what is final, to spend
the nights in staring at lit squares
of a thousand passing windows, a moth
with light-filled eyes and battered
body. So hesitate, because to know
what's best is only retrospective. Then go on.

I walk down the aisle until I see them,
can almost lose the distance
of the years, can almost feel
the old heat in their nearness . . .
I lurch against them as the train
quite suddenly starts up.
The steel shudders like a thing that feels,
as knights in some medieval battle
are terrified inside
their iron as they hurtle into air—
I see the seats
in which they sat are empty, dusty
as if they'd been unoccupied for years.
The car in which I ride is darkened
exactly like the one I left—except
the ticket stub that marked my stop
is missing from the clamp
above my chair. The good conductor
on his rounds must have removed it;
it means I'm free to leave
the speeding tunnel, and step
onto the ground that slows and stops,
into the lighted station
with the permissible exhaustion
of one who sees the sign above the platform—
the dozen letters that spell home.

                                    Philadelphia, 1979

See-Saw

Somewhere the balance shifts,
world's end that hung in air, in ozone
mist, begins to grow in weight;
the little puffed-up self goes up
almost like smoke, the earth
comes down on the other side
like rain. These are the gravities
of change, an apple dropped
into a pond, breaking the surface image
there, where all the self-regarding
kept their face.

In the beginning, then, the earth
seemed weightless in the air, an empty
sort of sphere, glimpsed by the rockets
as they soared, a crystal ball
that held the future, like an emerald seed, inside.

While, Cyclops on a stick, the telescope
of every private Palomar turned back
on itself and saw
a huge eye staring up, an eye
as red as Mars, as merciless.
Like a volcano in reverse, it drew
the whole world, flowing, to its cone—
a funnel that made everything go small
in passing through. And nothing
was enough—so great its appetite, so great
its gift for shrinking what it fed on.
It made the world into a crater; one look
could turn the sweetest flesh to stone.

And then, by laws as yet unstudied,
the eye began its slow dissolve
to grief—such rain
that all the stones began
to steam, the oldest tale retold,
the deluge with a different theme:
no wrathful God who chose one out
and drowned the rest, but *Shekhinah*
who wept for what was not and saved
the living with Her tears. And water-fed,
the crops came back, the earth began
to put on weight, the trees rose up
like steeples to the sky and birds came down
to feed and sing the summer into grass.
And over all, the arch of sun through rain,
the sign of healing sorrow
Shekhinah
whose covenant asks nothing
of tomorrow.

The End of the Line

The mind reels—
you feel the limits of the skull
holding the whirling cosmos in a thought,
the marching legions of the dead on a single circuit,
the bundle of nerves in the stalk of the brain
holding, like a Trajan's column,
the whole history of the race
wound and twisted
on the reel—
and the catch gives way
as the line pays out
when a marlin hits it
with such velocity it smokes
and the weak hands helpless
you can only pray
the line won't snap
and the great fish, blue and miraculous
as always, won't split the ocean's skin
and dive—

we've followed it so far

up the winding way from the salt caverns
into the blinding day, walking the weary nomad path
behind the grinding jaws of sheep,
seeding the even rows of fields
to the foot of the great stone keeps
rising to cloud-eaten turrets, the red silk wedge
of flags, the spikes of spires
driven into the midday air,
and the slow fall of dust into the crannies
when grass pulls down the stones again,
and the backs of trees broken
for ships, the blue fin of Asia beckons,
the ocean opened: the new world entered
by mistake—the line keeps paying out
the enormous blue writhing at the end
                                  as distant as ever
                    then, knowing you'll never
reel it back, that only in myth does the great thread
return to the spool and the weaving resume—
there comes the temptation
to reach for the knife

and cut the smoking line: the end
of tension and the aching in the arms,
the strained attention
and the gaping blue of what is out there waiting.

There is quiet now and the sweet lapping
of waves, no more tormented
by the thrashing in their heart . . .
only the ordinary breeze, the gentle tug
of tides, the amber light of late sun,
and far out, farther than the eye can track
or tired mind imagine
something blue as midnight,
            more powerful than hope,
swims free of our thin, killing line—

            leaping and sporting
lifting the water into the light: weightless
    windblown spray, a flower opening
        into mist, a fountain playing
                for the sake
                of play.

III. Requiems

Elegy for a Writer
for Judy

We met where people like us meet—
some seminar or other. She looked, at first,
all angles—like a drawing by a cubist,
hard lines that she preferred, the word
if it was raw, unsettled
as a country whose terrain is too forbidding
to invite the colonizers. She had no
small talk, and the man that year whom she
admired, she never spoke to. She had
the reticence of passion, the terror
of the early wounded, and the courage
of those who try to write their way
past repetition.
Of all her stories, I remember best
the one about the woman
who, as her love affair grew darker,
just this side of carnage, bought
yards and yards of yellow burlap
and hung it in the windows of her flat—
nothing fancy, but it changed the light.
However bleak, however stark
things were—I still can see her, on that
ladder, hanging bolts of yellow burlap
and challenging the odds.
She lived the next year in New York
and wrote for a cheap encyclopedia to eat
and spoke to no one. The job ran out at Z,
I saw her off to Europe; she said:
"I'm never going to live like this again."

When she came home, she moved and
took a lover, became a teacher, invited
friends for dinner—these simple things
for her were the invention
of the telegraph. And the daily sun
was always unexpected: it struck her
as it must have Noah, when the world
had gone, perhaps forever, in the rain.
And the dust that she ignored
to write her stories, played in the yellow
shafts of sun that hold the windows
up to the world outside. She wrote
another story: a mother, dying, calls her daughter
to her side, says: "Take care of your father."
The daughter takes her hand,
says "No!" in thunder,
in the best American tradition.

She died on the Arizona highways.
Her lover and I wept together, and like
a pair of thieves, crept into her apartment
to keep her journal and her stories
from her parents, from the hurt
of what was hers alone, that hard-won knowledge—
the outline of the trap that she had
sprung; that adamant, private
soul that she had salvaged
from the wreck. We met her parents at the airport;
they had her sleeping bag; we put it down between us.

Her father kept complaining
of the heat; he didn't like
anything we offered him to eat. He said
he hoped to find a life insurance policy
somewhere in her apartment, made out to him.
It had been a high speed, head-on collision;
her mother said the trooper told her
that her daughter had died instantly, but that
her heart had gone on beating
long after she was dead. I put my hands
up to my ears, and said I didn't want to hear that.
I hear it yet, that great heart beating,
and sometimes walking down a street
I think I see her—black hair, or something
in the walk, or in the angle of the cheek—
I start to call and then remember.

I have her stories, the latest versions,
with her own in-hand corrections,
in a manila envelope with a rusted metal clasp.
She had no patience with my elegant evasions,
she was never one for words to gloss
the facts. She would have said: dead loss
and sat down then to write and make it
final. If things are wrong
it's up to us at least to get it down
and get it right.

My Mother's Portrait
for Gertrude Sherby Rand 1913–1958

I

Those sumptuous, lacquered oils, a renaissance
begun too late, too many years waiting
for the children to grow, a husband
to come home to dinner, the sheets waiting
to be folded, those monograms of silk
a shimmer in the cupboard.
There was the silver to be shined
and lined up in the china closet,
the socks to be rolled and stored,
dark cashmere fists, in drawers.
So many years of lining shelves, the blue gleam
of washable paper, the polish on exquisite
French provincial, the clock's enamel face
ticking to the wall.

So when the canvases began
to glow with color, it was already so late,
so many centuries since the brush
was trained to follow the eye exactly, the slightest
glimmer of candlelight on a velvet drape,
a touch of ochre to a flushed pink cheek
soon to be varnished over, the elaborate gilt-edged
frames waiting, piled gaping against
the studio walls. So many people wanted to be painted;
unconsciously she flattered them, enhanced
the faces that she saw
with hazel eyes perhaps a shade too loving.

II

As the years, like brush strokes, built their patina
of early age, objects began to pile up
on the neat white space, became at last
a clutter: under the table, with its carved legs
and sculptured marble top, cramped space
began to fill, dissembled order, came more and more
to a confusion of brushes held, like a bouquet,
in a cup of India brass. The Renoir lady smiled forever
in her summer wicker chair. The precious little girl
copied from the cover of the Sunday magazine,
prim in mauve layers of gauze skirt, stood
with her black maryjanes catching the broken light
like the skin of lacquered eels. The soft blur
of pastel children's faces . . . the smell of fixative.
Some teacher who had tried to coax a freer form
but failed, had left a canvas of his own, an exercise
in flight, an explosion of birds, the sharp yellow
of beaks in a flurry of white feathers.

But the work stayed real in the old way, each detail
lovingly rendered and attended to, more and more
details, too much to remember, piling up
to a Victorian crescendo—no place
to breathe, the smoky vistas disappeared,
the foreground grew until it blotted out
even the pale *sfumato* of horizon.

III

Then her studio was empty, the paintings
portioned out to the remaining sisters.
And I don't know what happened to the half-squeezed
tubes of paint, the carefully cleaned brushes,
the little table with the marble top.
I don't know what happened to the years
it took the children to grow up in.
Nor how I could atone for that postponement,
those portraits piled up inside
like courtiers waiting
for an audience with an absent queen.

Sometimes I think for her that I continue—
break up the frames, disband the court, send home
the sycophants who want their likenesses enlarged,
announce, for her, an abdication . . .
and we go off together with our easels
to the open fields
where the birds wheel in the watercolor sky
and the crazy wheat walks blazing into autumn.

IV

I've only made another picture, tinted
the old print of a dream. Another mother
for the gallery of loss, that wall.
I need an instrument more blunt—
a palette knife to scrape away
these longings, scrape through, be done
with portraiture, soft words like that.
Scrape, scrape away until the light pours through.

And I'd let go those painted Russian dolls
that keep repeating themselves, smaller
each time, these images diminished by
regression, until they're nothing
but an eyeless button.
The snail's path, the winding roads of pearl,
turn back until one day they're finished.
Then the snail has her house and must move,
silver, on. Silent, feeding
on the leaves that give her cover.

Sometimes loss unravels slowly over years,
the old cord, the shed skin of a snake.
Those tribes where the navel cord
is left out in the sun to dry,
the wound to heal in a pucker of rose.
And the snake enters the grass
that has no path, no line can follow.
The brush turns silently to underbrush.
Everything loved is lost and free
to go its way, no tracks,
no turning
back, *visborach, v'yistabach, v'yispoar* . . .

Search Party
for Nancy Barnett Mack 1938–1975

The edges of the leaves are brown, lightly touched
by autumn. The sap's begun
its slow withdrawal into frost.
We were walking through the first of fallen leaves,
calling to the friend who'd wandered off,
calling as the gray sky darkened
toward the rain. Our call, and our approach,
unties a knot of birds
who scatter in a broken chord of cries.
Then, suddenly—it is too still,
as if the birds had chosen silence as disguise,
a silence so deceitful, so profound
the birds must be quite deafened by their hearts
beating against the fragile, thin-boned breasts
deep in the browning wood.

We go on calling for the one we lost. A friend
who must have turned off at a bend
and lost herself in cloud, or in the winding
autumn ways, obscured by leaves
not green nor yet quite gold,
somewhere in there where the birds play
dead.

As if all death were counterfeit,
all silence, sham—shattered by the racket of the heart:
give back, give back, give back
we shouted at the sky.
Then we heard something coming through the trees—
first with a rustle, then a rush, and then
an avalanche of rain.

And that, not us, first stirred
the birds to flight, then held them still:
a sky about to open,
a prayer about to be answered
by the air. So much
for the silence of the birds.
So much is given, and no more.

Postcard from the Great Southwest

See America First

That which has sense is not
by any stretch what once it was, these words
are small and flattened by addition
as a great stone cliff by years
and rain and slow attrition
begins to drift in bits
down its own sides—imagine
shedding tears made of the substance of
yourself, small grains dislodged
and sliding down the face until it's
changed, a photogenic sculpture for a while,
the whole shape finally shifts and falls
from the thousand little ruptures in the stone.

Down at the feet, a second shape begins, as if
the cliff could grow again. But this time it is made
of smaller stuff: the loose confederation
of the stones. As questions come from what
was certain once, the roots will break
the boulders up, the wind will shake
the staff of accident until
it bursts out in a green and leafy flourish
at the end. So rock is blurred, a forest
is begun, its fall assured. Things take
their time. The whole earth
slowly turns, like a tired village
at the fall of night, toward sleep . . .

the absolutely horizontal waits
side by side by side, the day
beyond a billion turns of sun,
the mountains at the level of the sea, the cliffs
worn down to common dust, thick
as coats of fur on a winter planet
in the evening of the sun, a flattened sphere
where falling light can find no lifted shape
to cast its shade, but just one plain, one vast
digression from some thought we were pursuing.
Beyond the tiny systems of the mind, an opening
where creatures brood and hatch
on planes that do not intersect with ours;
things without extremities, they slide
with such deliberate
ease, so slow they move beyond
our slight ability to see what moves at all.

Just the tireless line of the horizon, being
oozing out in no particular directions,
a slow osmosis
through distracted dust, the loss
of the exact, of separate skins, something
forever west of our distinctions—just
miles and miles and miles of sand, and
only one word needed: *and*
and *and* and *and* and *and* and . . .

The Literal = The Abstract:
A Demonstration

After all those swerving arcs in air,
the dance of shadows like an answer
from the ground, and all the dear
extravagance of flight, its sheering off
into delighted sky, where disappearing birds
with feathered script will spell
their life in flourishes
across a naked heaven . . .

as if the birds weren't there
to animate the skies, to dive
beneath the solid transience
of the bridges, the joy of water
in its rush to scatter
their reflections, a river moving
with its unseen weeds and fish,
all the unstated, understood
by context, as deer
surmised by thickets, or planets
missing in the moment of conjunction . . .

you may live forever and not see
a dead bird plummet down the chute
of sky, unless you have
a hunter by your side, his rifle
with its crossed-hair sight
to catch ellipsis on the wing
and turn it to a lump of bleeding feathers
falling at the same speed as a stone
in the perfect vacuum of the sky,
an elevator falling in the mind
where gravity is just equations
and the flight of birds
is only air in hollow bones, a concept
grasped by putting out its eyes.

The sun will send the birds
like notes from silver flutes into the air;
the gun
return them in a straight line
to your feet—the perfect absence
of what is absolutely there.

Caryatids
for Polly Iossifides

Once more there is the temptation
to be the cool gray fluted skirt,
the draped bodice of stone, the face
slightly worn away to mark
the sentence of time, the link
with the little mortal crouching in her
shade, and there, on top, the Ionic
capital: the last figure between
earth, pediment and the easy weight
of sky this poise supposes.

If you have not entered those
cool votaries of the porch
then you have not known
the horse breaking from the sea,
water streaming from the white cliffs of his teeth,
wrecks clinging to his coat like burrs.

If you have not taken the pose
that promises support without strain, something
unconditional—then
you have not felt the sea tugging at
the pebbles of your toes and known
the clouds of sulphur rising from the traffic
of the jerry-built metropolis below,
dismembering, grain by grain,
the cool marble of your composure.

If you have not felt the mad persuasion
of the world resting, like some temple,
on your head, then you have not heard
the sky falling
out toward the edge of comprehension, and collapsing,
a cloud of diamond dust, into the space
that cancels all equations.

If you have never seen the Western sunset stain
the marble of your last stand in gold, then
you have not seen the dragon rise from the waves
carrying its bellyful of maidens, and lick
and lick at the broken point
of Sounion, nor breathed the hot wind
blowing across from Africa, making the nerves
a red grid, a short circuit that ends
in a dazzle of ashes.

They are dismantling the hill—the crown
of ancient women, the aching cement in the temple wall.
In their place, they are going
to put up plaster, as if to set
the broken bones of a ghost.
Our children are dreaming of the species
that will come after us. This way to measure things
may not occur to us again. And this lament,

if lament it is, will soon seem quaint
as spinning wheels
turning, turning under the hand
of a fairytale crone mouldering
in the attic
of a castle
in a story
in a book
on a shelf
in a secondhand store
on a street
marked
for demolition.
The sun,
hung on its meridian—
a ball swung
from a crane, suddenly
begins its swing toward dark.

The Oldest Desire

And one is One, free in the tearing wind.

A woman, destitute, and taking cover
under the marble arch of winter, a monument
to some forgotten, bloody victory:
imagine a cheering crowd of red-cheeked
burghers, watching while the manacled
troop by, in the usual rags
of the losing side. The leaves look so
today, the old flags trodden underfoot.

Which is nature? The dim, retreating sun
that's lost another round, the shivering woman
muttering curses into her torn-off mittens
to keep her fingers warm? Or
the triumphant beauty of the ice
that silvers every pond and makes a filigree
of ferns and moss, rimed so artfully
with frost? It's cold, and nature's beauty
beggars nature. This constant casting off
of what has lost its hold, an insult
to those aching veins, half-clogged
with memory and regret, but carrying still
the living blood. If only they would stop
their cheering for the winners, stop
their staring. She's had enough of their
instructive nature—that blackboard where
the lecturing successful chalk their names.
The bootprints of a passing trapper—
the shallow graves for half a tribe of ants.
Her mind rejects the lesson. She thinks

about the fields around the house
where she remembers growing; some days
in winter when the ice had formed
its crust on top the snow and you could walk
for miles—light as you were—and leave
no track: the white as blank behind you
as before.

She wishes she were small again—so small,
a speck that could live crouched beneath a leaf,
unseen, all-seeing—a little bit of ticking life,
a sentient particle of dust, but bright: a spark
whose crumb of heat could set
a summer's worth of leaves
into a conflagration. And then,
oh then, how merry, and how warm—
the flames running red, licking like hell
over everything, set free in the tearing wind—
and never to be cold again, no, never.
Her fingers are red, they stiffen; the people
are staring again. But she's beyond them now, one
in a million dancing points of fire;
behind her, the blackened, burnt-out miles.

IV. Recoveries

Meditation on the Wēn-Fu

When the Heavenly Arrow is at its fleetest and sharpest,
what confusion is there that cannot be brought to order?

Lu Chi speaks of the heavenly arrow
and the sky parts. Quietly: not
with the flourish of trumpets, nor
with the clang of bronze doors thrown back, nor
with the velvet pomp of the lifting curtain—but
with the almost invisible shift of a cloud
that had obscured the sun, or the way
the dusk melts slowly into dark
and the stars ignite. This is not
the firing of the arrow, but merely
the drawing of heaven's bow.

It is hard to draw, and harder yet to say.
For this the brush had to be
invented, to speak in a wet rush like the living
tongue, moving over everything as a stream licks over
stones, in love with the feel of what
is opposite, or meeting another stream
with the lush music of affinity, or
after a long coursing through the rock beneath
the earth, it cries up
into the light, as a fountain.
As to the flowing and the not-flowing,
no one can explain it: how the spring
that gentled the earth with moss
and drew from it the delicacy of ferns
suddenly dries up
as if the voice of a god were stilled.

And the dead ferns rasp brittle underfoot,
the dry moss answers the hand with the scratch of briars,
making it a place now for the tourist,
for the disappointment of cameras. Though,
now and then, one comes who imagines
she hears in the sighing of wind in the dry weeds
some spirit released—a bird sprung from a trap.

While, in some unmarked spot, sacred
to no tribe—a trickle begins in the rocks, and,
in the slow way vision alters from below,
a pool takes shape like a quiet eye
to hold the heavens in its gaze, the sky
looking up through floating leaves,
having found its proper home.

And, as to the heavenly arrow
of which Lu Chi speaks—it must have struck
straight down, deep into stone, into the heart
of granite. Strange, then,
what wells up, what pours forth in a flood,
should be both clear and bright
as water, heavy and dark as blood;
that stone be wounded into speech
and that such wounds should heal us.

Ars Poetica

They wanted from us
loud despairs, ear-
splitting syntactical tricks, our guts
hung up to the light, privacy
dusted off and displayed, in ways
elliptical and clever, or
in a froth of spleen—details
of the damages, musings on divorce,
ashtrays from motels: films shot
on location, life made almost real
by its private dislocations. This,
they said, was the true
grit, the way it is, no lies, the heart
laid open as a pancake griddle to the awful
heat of rage, rage and desire, coiled beneath
and glowing, until even a drop of sweat
or ink, let fall in its vicinity,
would sizzle. And over all, the big I
swollen like a jellyfish, quivering
and venomous. These things were
our imperative: the poet
in his stained T-shirt, all gripes
and belly, and, well, so *personable*—
my god, so like ourselves!
Oh yes, the women poets too, so
unashamed, ripping off their masks
like nylon stockings.

*   *   *

And all the time, the shy and shapely
mind, like some Eurydice, wanders—
darkened by veils, a shade
with measured footsteps. So many things are gone
and the end of the world looms
like a shark's fin on the flats of our horizon.
Fatigue sets in, and the wind rises.
The door is swinging on its hinges—the room
pried open, the one upstairs in Bluebeard's castle.
They have been hanging there a long time
in their bridal dresses, from hooks,
by their own long hair.
The wind that makes them sway until
they seem almost alive
is like the rush of our compassion.
Yes, now we remember them all
and the sea with its unchanging heaving—a grief
as deep and as dactylic as the voice of Homer,
and, as we turn another way, we lay the past out
on Achilles' shield, abandon it to earth,
our common ground—the bridal hope, its murder,
the old, old story, perpetual
as caring: the scant human store
that is so strangely self-restoring
and whose sufficiency
is our continual surprise.

The Daughters of Midas

Gold.
The word is a struck bell, resounds
as light rays out from a gold-chased cup, full
to the brim with sun and spilling
molten gold that hardens when it's plunged, hissing
into the tub, as living sap turns amber
in the lake—the tears of Phaëton's sisters,
who never drove the chariot of the sun, but
stopped to see their brother's fire
quenched: men dream of falling, women
of growing hard and rooted to the ground.
The trees shed amber tears, so gold
their grief, so unconsoling.
But there were others—more like us, dark
flies in amber, trapped another way,
a curious imperfection, caught in the tears
of dutiful sisters: through a haze of gold
we saw a world we couldn't touch.

But that seems centuries ago . . . those statues
of a golden age, standing in a royal hall,
their hands held out—imploring, waiting
for a change of heart, of father,
a hunger that could take him
to the river. Those sands have been gold
a long time now, the river filled
with different water, rising—

as if Persephone had risen, the first
forsythia, whose gold no god could catch, nor stay
its blooming, bursts into flower; by summer,
when the sun has touched our skins
with gold, no one can tell us
in the rich fields where we walk, from wheat,
nor wheat from water.

Labyrinth

sila ersinarsinivdluge

You've lost the clue—somewhere
in the maze, the golden thread's
run out . . . and the air
is getting thick and grainy as old film,
filling with something foul and dank
as steam rising in the heat
from a heap of compost: the animal's lair
is just ahead, the thread's out,
you'll have to go it alone and chance
what's there. The walls have narrowed
to a channel, damp to the hands
that grope your way; the rank air
hangs against the stone, as if
the stone had hooks and held it.
You can't stay where you stand; in the dark
ahead you hear the snorting
and the dull report of hoofs
moved restlessly in place, and then
the corner's rounded. You feel it first
before you see it, and know you've found
the chamber. It is a widening in the stone
lit by a feeble light
that's lost its force from filtering
down the deep rock chimney
from the sky, a sky that's so remote
it's dwindled to this sickly glimmer.
The floor that opens out around you
is spread with straw, in places worn almost
to dust that rises from the ground
where something stamps and stumbles
in its place; the cloud obscures
its shape, postpones
the moment when you'll have to face it.

As a beast will suddenly stiffen at the scent
of someone unexpectedly about, there is
the silence of held breath, a slow settle
of the dust. Just so it appears, as if
a mist had risen and the moon come out.
You both stand frozen for a moment—
two pairs of eyes take hold
and widen, each to take the other in.

The beast is the color of turning cream,
slender with a fawn's grace, fragile
as gentleness grown old, its large eyes
soft with sorrow, its horns
are ivory candelabra, its worn flanks
scarred with roads like countryside
seen from the air. It neither shrinks back
nor approaches, but waits, as snow just fallen
waits for the wind to shape it to the land.
So, slowly you approach, extend your hand and
let the soft nose sniff it, then touch the velvet
muzzle as you touch a rose, wanting to know
its silk but not to bruise it. And then
you know, and turn to go, and hear the light foot
falls that follow yours and never falter,
only pausing where you pause
as branching way leads on to way. Somewhere near
you hear the sound of dripping water, slow
and even over stone. You feel a nuzzle
at your shoulder, as if to say
this way, go on. So, sometimes led
and sometimes leading, you go until you feel

the air grow fresher, and there's a filament
of light, a slow unravel of gold
like a ray of sun as it passes through the water.
A moment later, the two of you step
blinking into the shining day.

We stood high above the tree line
where the glacier's edge, touched by sun,
becomes a maze of running streams,
a million veins of silver opened into summer.
We stood a long time there amazed
before we felt the bite of hunger and,
together with the sun, began the long climb down.

Running Out

And we were always, I suppose, sorry
for the way that things worked out,
a silver river run over
by its banks, until it was the merest thread,
the residue of lace.
We sit here with our reed poles resting
on the pylons, fishing in desultory fashion,
like those who know the local stream's fished out
but still enjoy the cool charade
of meditation, the bright bait
in its little plastic boxes. The years pile up
like sandbags by a channel
that hasn't known a flood since
it grew small. Some took it all
as a matter of course, the usual dwindling
of a rich resource, the pay-off.

While some took nature otherwise—
a course in matter, read dappled light
in wooded clearings, filtered through
the green of wind-stirred leaves.
The eaves were eloquent
with nesting birds, and bright
the sun-soaked fields, the yellow sheaves
of wheat. All this inflated hopes
made poor, dry repetition made
cliché, and made us sorry for
the way that things run out:
the dried-up stream down to a trickle
like spittle down the slack
mouth of the old and the afflicted.

However old, we're children
in the heart of winter,
faces pressed against the glass;
the cold outside will turn
our breath to water at the last,
the long streaks on the pane
like tears we don't remember shedding.
Outside, those voices
that we can't decipher, rising
in the ear and falling, are
the streams new-filling—running over,
running out of rock.

Reading Frankenstein *at the Equator*

A lightning burst like a strobe-light flash:
a moored ship in a frozen bay.
Two figures flee across the ice
in silhouette, a dark pursuit.
From here, where we live without shadows,
it is impossible to tell
the monster from the man. To us
they both look equal, real as hell.
And which one made the other, as she thought,
from rejected parts and the buried red
of the heart? Anyone's guess.

Beside us in this steaming place
where green is close to black and leaves drip lazily
into the glowing stream—the oldest infant,
pink, unblushing, fat, fires his arrows
into the swirling pools
where they seem to swim like watersnakes
in a delirious tangle. Here, where light is
everywhere, the dense green line of vegetation
draws the world together: the dark
sweet fetor of the earth and the blue
exhaust fumes of the plants and the black
where space begins and new worlds sleep,
curled like lovers in each other's dreams,
waiting to be wakened. The arrows swim,
electric eels, blinded by their own
discharge of lightning, stirring
the soup that sends things sliding through the ooze
who feel their life along their sides
like some beginning Adam. They wake
and shake the morning from their flanks:

everything stirs, the bird in the back
of the lizard's mind, the man uncurls
in the monkey's paw, and deep in the recess
of the human brain, what strange creation
wakens? We stretch and face
our future with a yawn, as each dawn brings
some fresh exhaustion; as the exhaling plants
gave us our atmosphere for breathing,
may we leave something precious
for what follows
from our exchange with light.

Though a golden swarm of bees in the old,
arranging sun may seem
mere dazzle in the snow-blind eyes
of that pair in the polar regions who pursue
each other over the glacier's razored top—
we keep the hope, here under
the mile-high ferns, that the race will end
with their embrace—and a single figure
will emerge, take ship for a warmer place.

Recovery

Hercules, his muscles useless now
as sculpture, puts down the giant
on the earth that he had strangled
in the air. And leaves him there for dead, going on
to enter legend, another weight-lifter
with an inflated reputation, his cradle
with the strangled snakes still in it
in the attic with the toys he had outgrown.

Antaeus stirred, and groaned.
He gathered his limbs, like something
he had spilled, and slowly rose
and stood—as large as ever, his dew-soaked hair
rubbing the highest branches of the trees.
How many years he had been lying there
he didn't know, how many winters
laid their snow across his inert flesh
he had forgotten—the centuries
were like a dream that faded with his waking,
the last thing that he knew was not
the first thing he remembered—
                                        Hercules,
the earth as it receded,
the awful blank when everything went
blue, the insubstantial blue in which he drowned,
unconscious and celestial, the freezing air.
He felt the vertigo again, blue thinning
to a white so absolute it was pure
absence . . . and then he shook his head
as if to clear it—the birds took flight, and the clouds
parted. He felt the sun on the slopes
of his shoulders and his back,

the earth still under his feet.
He had no name for what he felt,
though some of it was grief for the lost
years, for all that might have been
and might be yet. And he wept as giants weep
and water planets. In the rain he heard them
calling—the dead, or the children born
while he was waking. He seemed to hear his name
in the rustling of a thousand leaves:
Antaeus, Antaeus, Antaeus.

And even in the distant towns, on islands
where the freighters seldom call—they heard him
coming. Even the patients, numb
on the silver tables, stirred, and stillborn
babies opened their lungs and yelled.
Dumb oxen looked up from their grazing
and power lines hummed in the air.
Somewhere in space, its mission aborted,
a capsule and its crew made their reentry—
those, who when they thought themselves lost,
could only think to go off automatic, take control
and turn the dials to another setting—back
to the sweet and clouded curve of space
that shelters earth: as it grew
larger in their portholes, the glass
blazed blue, and soon they felt—
as infants must, the moment
before birth—the heave
of ocean under them
and under that,
the earth.

Desertsong

(Meditation on a Dance by Jeff Duncan)

I brush my hair and it swings out
in air, black water falling
down the canyon wall. A breeze turns left
and lifts it into silver
spray, as years and wind have lifted me
in my slow fall and put this silver
in my hair. It is thick in my fingers
as I twist it into braids, I think
how many times I've drawn it
in by day and let it down
to welcome night, the moon lacing its black
with glinting threads of gray, and I
am woven into night the way
a reed is woven in this basket whose dark mouth
overflows with silver fish, those stars
I've bent and netted from the stream.
And oh, though I am woven in, I swear,
I am light as a reed that sways in the gentlest air
by the river in the deepest canyon's shade.
I who stood once as a cactus stands, bristling
in the sun, and I was hard to those who, thirsty,
passed, and from my earthbaked water jar,
I offered none. And stood unmoved
while my shadow crept around me, dark
on the sun dial of the sand, marking time.

It's hard to say which day, or what, began the dance.
Was it the slow processional
of ants, or the spider
who stepped its many legs, impeccable,
deliberate, through the sand? Or a beetle
scurrying with its black shield on its back,
a pair of twig-like sticks so sensitive they catch
the rumor of a gnat, the breathing
of a flea, mosquito whine, the jerk
of a butterfly's wing? It was the slightest
thing. A pebble for an avalanche.
And like the ancient ones who left
the stones behind so they could travel light—
I was unburdened of such weight
the earth came easy to my feet
as flight comes to the heron or the bat.
Now, as I dance, the light stops where I am,
I cast a weaving shadow for the gnats
who gather, lively, in my shade; my dark side
comforts them and I am glad
to dance the afternoon away, and leave
a trail like sanskrit in the sand, old words
the wind will soon efface, the water falling
through the air, while on their mounds
the prairie dogs keep watch
in silence as intense as prayer.

In Medias Res

Here we are in the midst of things—
the same longings
for a body that would last, the same
slow breaking down of what we are
and learn to love and lose:

there are no fathers in the sky,
no mothers in the earth—for who, if he had
fathered men, would twist them till
they're bent with time as olive trees
that, as they grow more picturesque,
begin to bear hard fruit? And who, being
mother to another being would
give it a taste of life, then, yawning
take it back again?

And who's the fool who sexed the stars,
fixed tyrants in the sky—anointed
the staring sun as if it were a king,
appointed the cold moon
a virgin queen, dragging the helpless sea
behind her like a train of panting suitors?
And set the stumbling history of a race
into celestial stone? So that we have to pray
a comet down to rid ourselves of those
whose madness put them on the throne,
who buy with a legion's death
a night or two of feasting in a rented hall.

Who goes there weeping at the vast
inhuman panoply of stars? Or mourns the passing
of the gods who, if something like ourselves,
are more corrupt than any drought
that merely signifies the absence of the rain.

Today then let us build a temple to the stars
we see above us now, burned out
ten million years ago; hosannahs
to the wind that shifts the silent dunes
without intent; and amen to the deep rot
of the forest floor, the subatomic world
we'll never see, the sweet collisions
and the million accidents of time
that gave us life—and all those miracles,
indifferent and inhuman as the waves
that Adam in his garden never dreamed
because they're no more kin
to him than heaven is to kings
or what is natural to what is named.

For what we love we can't call
names—what calls to us
in *medias res*, that thick green sedge
by the river, and we suppose it
as a bird, though what it is, is
singing.

The Continuous is Broken, and Resumes

Adam made the world
stand still so he could name it: the woods
intelligible as thought expressed
in leaves, and when they would not stay
forever green, he took the fall
and turned its gold to parable. And the long slither
of the snake became his dread
uncoiling in the grass. And when, obsessively, the same
thought kept repeating in his head
and in his ears, the trees filled up with locusts
throbbing—so shrill the birds
took off. The rock was his fixed idea;
the creation, to continue, required
his attention. The seasons he made gods
and, as the storms announcing spring
tear limb from limb, the holy ground
was smirched with blood to breed
the soft uncurl of seedlings. This murder
he called Orpheus, Dionysus, Jesus. Man
set it going, his matins
made the sun come up; if he forgot to dance,
the rain grew stubborn. His sin
had such effect that it could blight
the earth, bring on eclipse, rot the fruit
before it ripened. The great god he created
walked among the tents, his sandals opened
fissures in the ground, his touch
made the hills smoke. When Adam slept
the world grew still, mute as a great
organ whose towering pipes require
a little pair of hands
to move the air in thunder.
And how he dreamed of closure: obsessed
with falling curtains, heroic couplets,
and the absolute chord of amens.

Now everywhere he walks, the world is mute.

When he has passed, the birds pick up the notes
where they had dropped them, the wind begins again
to call soft speech from the leaves,
and the deer, seeing the woods deserted
by all but the sea-green light,
walk out into the clearing.
And the ocean nearing the shore
heaves a sigh of relief
and a great shudder goes through the swells,
as when a wind lightly passes.
And the sun, as the earth turns by it,
writes its changing shadows on the land.
Everything speaks of itself:
the fireflies in their code of light—
short flashes, the long dark in between;
the sand, grain by grain, is a pure reiteration;
the earth takes up again its ceaseless
conversation, picking up where it left off—
as a stream, after the agitation of the rapids,
where it was interrupted by the rocks,
flows on again, lyrical
as laughter, with the sheer delight
that can't be called indifference,
without the least concern for whether
anyone is out there, listening.

Ex Libris

By the stream, where the ground is soft
and gives, under the slightest pressure—even
the fly would leave its footprint here
and the paw of the shrew the crescent
of its claws like the strokes of a chisel
in clay, where the lightest chill, lighter
than the least rumor of winter, sets the reeds
to a kind of speaking, and a single drop of rain
leaves a crater to catch the first silver
glint of sun when the clouds slide away
from each other like two tired lovers,
and the light returns, pale, though brightened
by the last chapter of late autumn:
copper, rusted oak, gold aspen, and the red
pages of maple, the wind leafing through to the end
the annals of beech, the slim volumes
of birch, the elegant script of the ferns . . .

for the birds, it is all
notations for a coda, for the otter
an invitation to the river,
and for the deer—a dream
in which to disappear, light-footed
on the still open book of earth,
adding the marks of their passage,
adding it all in, waiting only
for the first thick flurry of snowflakes
for cover, soft cover that carries
no title, no name.

Notes

Shekhinah: Jewish theology—A cloud of glory resting between the cherubim on the mercy-seat in the tabernacle, as the symbol of the divine presence; a word not found in the Bible but adopted from the Targum by Christians. In the Talmudic and Midrashic literature the same general concept is developed. It is believed that the Shekhinah took up its abode in the tabernacle from the day of its erection and moved wherever the tabernacle went until the temple of Solomon was built, where it remained until the exile, when, according to some, it went with the deported Jews, while others maintained that it returned to heaven. At any rate, it was not in the second temple. Later Jewish piety held a variety of views as to the nature of the Shekhinah, from the concept of an immanent presence everywhere in the world to that of an independent entity standing between God and the world. (*Funk & Wagnall's New Standard Dictionary of the English Language,* 1938.)

1. According to tradition, all references to the Shekhinah, the feminine and indwelling aspect of the sacred, were expunged from the ancient writings when they were made canonical in the Old Testament of the partriarchs. The concept returns and figures prominently in the Zohar, a Jewish mystical text probably written in thirteenth-century Spain. According to Carol Ochs, the Zohar, a commentary on and reinterpretation of the first five books of the Bible, contained for those who held it sacred "something they had not found in traditional Judaism. . . . A study of the Zohar should tell us what was missing in Rabbinic Judaism." Among the missing attributes the Zohar attempts to restore to the sacred is the Shekhinah: " 'Shekhinah,' a feminine gender word, derived from the Hebrew verb *shakhan* ('the act of dwelling'), was used in post-Biblical times to denote the physical manifestation of God's presence. . . . The Zohar's emphasis on the Shekhinah as the feminine element, opposed to the masculine aspect of God, responded to a deep-seated religious need. The Shekhinah became the loving, motherly, suffering,

mourning aspect of Deity who went into exile with the people of Israel and would remain with them. . . . " ("The Feminization of Judaism in the Zohar," *Behind the Sex of God: Toward a New Consciousness—Transcending Matriarchy and Patriarchy* [Boston: Beacon Press, 1977]).

2. "Emigration": The Mary Taylor who was Charlotte Brontë's friend closely resembles the figure in the poem, though I have taken two liberties with the facts. The original Mary Taylor emigrated, not to Australia, but to New Zealand. Since Taylor sounds better with Australia and the point, after all, is the same, I correct the record here and leave the poem alone. The other divergence from fact results from literary biography's loss of interest in Mary Taylor after the date of her famous friend's death. No one much marks that in 1860, five years after Charlotte Brontë died, Mary Taylor returned to England at the age of 46, nor did I know it when I wrote the poem. I prefer to go on thinking of her living on "to a great old age" in "Australia." In fact, she did not reenter English society when she returned to England, but kept to herself in a final independence. This, to my mind, rhymes in sense with the liberty the poem takes with (and gets from) her life.

3. "Cancelling the Space Program": The madhouse on the slopes of Mt. Olympus is more than a trope; it is a fact.

4. "Candied": This poem is heavily indebted to a delightful poem on a similar theme by Mary Hesky.

5. "A Short History of Philosophy": A contributing source to this poem (which I realized only after I'd written it) is James Agee's last letter to Father Flye, a letter never mailed but found—stamped and addressed—on Agee's mantel after his death. The peculiarly affecting pathos of his elephant movie scenario stayed with me. The text can be found in *Letters of James Agee to Father Flye* (New York: George Braziller, 1962). Any resemblance of the elephant to Wallace Stevens is coincidental, though not purely so. The lines "He was the one who moved

and, moving, made/the world around him run" are a travesty echo of the lines from Stevens's "The Idea of Order at Key West": "there never was a world for her/Except the one she sang and, singing, made."

6. "Desertsong": This poem follows the movements of a dance called "La Mesa del Brujo" ("The Sorcerer's Plateau"), 1979, choreographed and danced by Jeff Duncan to "Songs from the Hill" by Meredith Monk.